Stretching Basics

The Body Coach Series

Stretching Basics

Stretching & Flexibility for Sport,

Lifestyle and Injury Prevention with

Australia's Body Coach®

Paul Collins

Meyer & Meyer Sports

British Library Cataloguing in Publication Data
A catalogue record for this book is available from the British Library

Paul Collins
Stretching Basics
Oxford: Meyer & Meyer Sport (UK) Ltd., 2007
ISBN 978-1-84126-220-8

© 2007 by Meyer & Meyer Sport (UK) Ltd.
Aachen, Adelaide, Auckland, Budapest, Graz, Indianapolis, Johannesburg, New York,
Olten (CH), Oxford, Singapore, Toronto
Member of the World
Sport Publishers' Association (WSPA)
www.w-s-p-a.org

Printed and bound by: B.O.S.S Druck und Medien GmbH, Germany
ISBN 978-1-84126-220-8
E-Mail: verlag@m-m-sports.com
www.m-m-sports.com

Introduction

Welcome!

I'm The Body Coach, Paul Collins your exclusive personal coach here to guide and motivate towards improving your flexibility. *Stretching Basics* provides an introductory guideline to stretching and flexibility exercises for sport, lifestyle and injury prevention.

Stretching before and after work, exercise or sport plays a vital role towards keeping muscles pliable, flexible and free of tension. Most importantly, everyone can stretch, regardless of age or flexibility or lack of. It doesn't matter whether you are a professional athlete or tradesperson, an office worker or parent; the same general principles of stretching apply for everyone.

Stretching is an important part of living. It helps keep muscles supple and allows you to keep in touch with your body so each day you feel fresh and invigorated. Stretching also helps prepare your body for movement, then afterwards in helping warm down the body. To provide you with a benchmark of your where you currently stand in terms of your flexibility, I have established eight benchmark testing exercises.

I would also like to introduce the revolutionary Passive Muscle Assessment or PMA which allows you to gauge, pin-point and release specific muscular trigger points around the body (using a Muscle Mate®) as well as provide you with a series of Dynamic Warm-up exercises you can perform whilst on the move.

In addition, *Stretching Basics* is packed with over 60 stretches grouped into specific muscle categories for ease of selection, as well as a series of stretching routines for sport, work and play guaranteed to improve your muscular flexibility and range of motion.

I look forward to working with you!
Paul Collins
The Body Coach

Contents

Introduction 5

About the Author 8

Chapter 1 Introduction to Stretching 9

Chapter 2 Testing Flexibility and Range of Motion 15

Chapter 3 Passive Muscle Assessment (PMA) 24

Chapter 4 Dynamic Warm-up – Stretching on the Move . . .32

Chapter 5 Quadriceps and Anterior Hip Muscles 39

Chapter 6 Hamstrings 48

Chapter 7 Lower Limb 58

Chapter 8 Adductors (groin) .66

Chapter 9 Gluteal (buttock) and Hip Region 73

Chapter 10 Hip, Pelvic and Lumbar Region 81

Chapter 11 Iliotibial Band (ITB) and Sacroiliac Joint 91

Chapter 12 Upper Body Region 98

Chapter 13 General Stretching Routines 115

       • Passive Muscle Assessment (PMA) 116

       • Reducing Lower Back Tension 118

       • Pre-and-Post Work Stretching Routine 120

       • 3-Minute Office Stretching Routine 122

Chapter 14 Sports Specific Stretching Routines 123

       • General Sports Stretching Routine 125

       • Ball Sports 126

       • Balance Sports .128

       • Golf Specific .130

       • Martial Arts .132

       • Racquet and Bat Sports 134

       • Running Specific 136

       • Swimming Specific 138

Stretching Index 141

About the Author

Paul Collins is an Award-winning Personal Trainer in Australia, a prolific author on fitness and weight loss topics and General Manager of the Australian Academy of Sport and Fitness; an International College in Sydney, Australia specifically for overseas students wishing to study and obtain Fitness and Personal Training qualifications. Each year Paul inspires thousands of people through appearances on TV, Radio, Print Media and seminars.

Coaching since age 14, Paul has personally trained world-class athletes and teams in a variety of sports, e.g., athletics, rugby, soccer, squash, tennis and many others including members of the Australian Olympic Swimming Team. He is also a key presenter to the Australian Track and Field Coaching Association, Australia Swimming Coaches and Teachers Association, NSW Squash Academy and the Australian Fitness Industry. Paul is an outstanding athlete is his own right, having played grade level in the national rugby league. He is also a former Australian Budokan Karate Champion, A-grade Squash Player and NSW Masters Athletics Track & Field State Champion.

As a leader in the field of personal fitness and weight loss, Paul has successfully combined a sports fitness background with a Bachelor of Physical Education Degree and international certification as a Strength and Conditioning Coach and Personal Trainer. As designer of *The Body Coach* book series, exercise products and educational programs, Paul travels internationally to present a highly entertaining series of corporate Health & Wellbeing Seminars and exclusive Five-star Personal Training for VIPs.

www.thebodycoach.com

For more details visit: www.thebodycoach.com

Chapter 1
Introduction to Stretching

Stretching is for everyone. Observe your friendly K-9 or household cat and you'll notice them instinctively stretching throughout the day. Their methods are gentle and easy and we can learn from this. As humans, stretching can be performed at anytime throughout the day also – at work, waiting for a bus, even after sitting or standing for long periods as a form of muscular relief of tension. Animals stretch regularly and so should we. The major benefit we have over our friendly pets is the luxury of a shower to warm the muscles. From experience, a warm shower provides the heat and elasticity in the muscle for peaceful and relaxing stretch afterwards, morning or evening. Otherwise a gentle build up of exercise or physical activity for 5 minutes is used to warm the muscles and increase blood flow before stretching. It's also a good idea to stretch after exercise or sport to reduce muscle soreness the following day.

Stretching itself can be a routine to prepare you for work or allowing a transition from low-level exercise to more vigorous movement or sport. Stretching isn't about how far your can bend or move a limb, it's simply a way of keeping the body more supple and maintaining range of motion, which helps reduce the risk of injury. If you are healthy you can learn how to stretch safely and enjoy the benefits of Stretching Basics.

Benefits of Stretching

Stretching plays a vital role in preparing your body for activity or sport. It also plays a vital role after exercise, as part of a warm down in order to keep muscle and joints supple, flexible and free of tension. For this reason it is essential to understand the right techniques and what stretches work for you.

Some benefits of stretching include:
- Reduced muscular soreness and tension
- Enhanced circulation
- Improved body awareness and muscular co-ordination
- Making the body feel relaxed, yet invigorated
- Good range of motion and pliability of muscles and joints

THE BODY COACH

- Assisting in the development and maintenance of flexibility
- Reduced risk of injury to joints, muscles, and tendons

Who Can Benefit from Stretching

Age is no barrier when it comes to stretching. Stretching can help maintain flexibility, which may otherwise decline with age or inactivity due to an injury. Exercises themselves can be modified to suit everyone's needs. In order to keep the body aligned and reduce the risk of injury you will need to pay attention to your posture and body positioning throughout each exercise. Athletes who maintain a good range of movement of joints and muscles can benefit by being able to maintain optimal range during physical activity. On the other hand, stretching can benefit people involved in a stationary occupation such as a computer operator or driver whose muscles tend to shorten from lack of use. Whichever the case, regular stretching can help maintain good posture and reduce lower back and neck tension. Individuals with certain muscular imbalances or postural problems can benefit from stretching, but always see your doctor and physiotherapist for approval prior to starting any exercise or stretching program.

Warm up the Muscles First

One of the most important elements to introduce is that muscles should be warm when stretched. The best time to stretch is when your heart rate and body temperature has increased, such as after a warm shower or build-up in physical activity levels by performing some type of brief aerobic activity (5–10 minutes) such as walking, light jogging or skipping. This ensures the muscles and tendons are more pliable and blood is circulating around the body quicker to the working muscles.

Skipping is a great way to warm-up the body

Warming Down after Physical Activity

After physical activity or sport, the best way to reduce muscle fatigue and soreness is through light activity, such as walking forwards, sideways and backwards, followed by stretching. Introduce a 10-15 minute warm down after exercise or playing sport to maintain range of motion and reduce muscle soreness. A regular stretching routine after physical activity is good practice. It will not only make you feel better, but will also reduce muscle soreness the following day.

Static Stretching

Once a warm-up has been performed, the body temperature has increased and the muscles are more elastic. This allows the body stretch more efficiently in a static position – no bouncing! Static stretching itself consists of stretching a muscle (or group of muscles) towards their end range, ensuring good posture, technique and no pain, and then maintaining or holding that position for a set period of time. For example, in a sitting position reaching forwards from your hips to touch your toes. The goal when stretching is ensuring correct technique and good posture is maintained at all times. Picture yourself as a dancer holding a nice long body position and excellent posture whilst stretching, as this is the focus required to gain the benefits of stretching.

Holding a Stretch

For general use, a static stretch may be held for up to 15 seconds or longer. It is a slow and gentle stretch, without tension or pain. One of the reasons for holding a stretch for a prolonged period of time is that the muscle group becomes accustomed to its new length. Through regular stretching sessions you can gradually train the muscles stretch receptors to allow greater lengthening of the muscles and become more flexible. On the other hand, persons who are hypermobile or have excessive range of joint motion need to ensure stability of joints as opposed to flexibility.

THE BODY COACH

To maintain focus on your body position and the task at hand, it is good practice to maintain a deep breathing pattern whilst counting the time on task out loud (or in your mind). Each stretch may be completed in sets of 2–5 repetitions on both sides of the body, with a short rest in between each stretch.

Always hold a stretch in a comfortable position rather than strain or overstressing the muscle. If you are experiencing discomfort, pain or tension before, during or after stretching you should discontinue stretching and seek appropriate medical advice to help identify the cause and rectify the problem.

Getting Started

The best feature about stretching is that it's free and can be performed anytime, anywhere (home, gym, work, sports or training) after a good warm-up. Stretching should be gentle and performed regularly with an understanding that it takes time (months, sometimes years) for your muscles, tendons, ligaments and joints to adjust, especially if your goal is to increase flexibility. For the regular exerciser and athlete stretching in-between training sessions, playing sport or competition helps keep the muscle fresh and free of tension. On the other hand, the office worker has the opportunity to stretch various muscles groups throughout the day to release any tension.

When starting out you need to take it slowly, breathe deeply and stretch gently with your attention focused on maintaining good posture on the specific muscles being targeted. Your breathing should remain deep and controlled.

In the following chapters a series of basic stretching exercises are demonstrated for the whole body. These stretches can be used individually or collectively as a group. Then, in the final chapter of this book you'll find a number of sample stretching routines for sport, work and play.

Getting to Know Your Body

The following diagram helps demonstrate various muscle regions for stretching.

Front View

Rear View

Biceps

Neck

Triceps

Forearm

Upper Back

Lower Back

Quadriceps

Gluteals (butt)

Illiotibial Band

Hamstrings

Calves

Adductors

THE BODY COACH

Chapter 2

Testing Flexibility and Range of Motion

Assessing your flexibility, joint range of motion and stability plays an important role in the types of stretches you perform. Some areas of the body for instance may be tense or restricted whilst other areas may be weak or hypermobile. A tight area of the body may require regular stretching, massage and physical therapy treatment whereas a weak, loose or hypermobile joint or series of joints may require strength and stability exercises as opposed to stretching. This is because stretching a joint that is hypermobile can make it more unstable. If this is the case, working with a physical therapist to help strengthen these areas is a priority for you.

The ultimate goal of a stretching program is finding muscular balance throughout the body that suits your lifestyle by finding out your strengths and weaknesses. The following tests will help guide you with improving awareness of your body and the balance between muscle groups. Ensure you have performed an appropriate warm-up prior to stretching. Never force a stretch or work with pain as it only leads to injury. Instead, focus on working in a comfortable movement range. Use these and other stretches as benchmarks for improvement. A regular stretching plan should form part of a daily lifestyle plan as it prepares your body and mind for work, physical activity, sport or play.

1   Triceps

Description
Right Side

- Raise the right arm and place hand behind neck
- Reach with left arm up behind body
- Can you clasp hands?

Left Side

- Raise the left arm and place hand behind neck
- Reach with right arm up behind body
- Can you clasp hands?

Groin

Description

- Sit with knees out to the side and soles of feet together
- Place your elbows on your knees and clasp your ankles with your hands
- Gently push knees towards the ground to find your end range
- How far do your legs lower down?

Wall Slide

Description

- Step legs out from wall with feet shoulder width apart
- Bend knees and sit with back kept against the wall
- Raise both arms to the side at 90-degree angle and make contact with wall
- Slowly raise both arms up maintaining contact with wall until arms straight overhead
- Do you feel any restrictions when raising arms? For instance, does your lower back arch or do you find it hard to maintain the arms against the wall raising or lowering

Note: *This test is particularly important for swimmers for maintaining a streamline body position.*

4 Spine Rotation

Description

- Stand sideways to wall arms length away
- Raise both arms forward parallel to ground
- Keeping feet shoulder-width apart and facing forwards gently rotate arms and shoulders to the side (as shown) in a coordinated motion
- Keep head facing forwards
- Do you feel any tension, unevenness or restriction in rotation?
- Repeat facing opposite direction

Note: *This test is particularly important for rotational sports or activities such as golf or baseball to ensure good body rotation*

Phase 1 Phase 2

Description

Phase 1
- Sit on ground and grab the sole of foot with hand
- Straighten leg whilst keeping body upright
- Can you straighten the leg or are there restrictions?
- Repeat with opposite leg?

Phase 2
- Grab the sole of both feet
- Extend and straighten one leg
- Maintaining balance of the body, extend the other leg
- Can you straighten both legs and maintain balance?
- Repeat with opposite leg?

Note: *This test is particularly important for sports and activities that require flexibility, balance and strength such as dancing, gymnastics and martial arts*

Adductors – Side Splits

Description

- Place hands on floor and spread legs wide keeping chest parallel to ground
- Point toes forwards 45-degrees and roll onto inside of foot to increase stretch angle
- Spread legs out to side to end range, without pain
- How far can you lower down?

Note: *This test is particularly important for dance, gymnastic and martial arts orientated sports*

Description

- Extend one leg forward and the opposite leg back
- Lower body towards ground to see what angle you can achieve
- Work within limits – avoid overstretching
- How far can you lower?
- Repeat stretch with opposite leg forward
- Does one side lower further than the other?

Note: *This test is particularly important for dance, gymnastic and martial arts orientated sports*

Description

- Stand tall with feet one and a half shoulder-widths apart and arms crossed in front of body parallel to ground
- Lower and raise body slowly by simultaneously bending at the hip, knee and ankle region
- Maintain good body alignment – line from ear through shoulder, knee and ankle (lateral view)

THE BODY COACH

Key Points

- Is you body weight across your foot print, without feet rolling inwards?
- Is your knee alignment over middle toes?
- Do your knees roll inwards or heels lift from the ground (poor form)?
- Can you lower to 90-degree leg angle without loss of form?

Note: *This test is particularly important for all sports and activities that require running, jumping, lifting and carrying. A good squat ensures effective hip and leg strength, good body alignment and stability is acquired.*

Chapter 3

Passive Muscle Assessment (PMA)

Passive Muscle Assessment or PMA plays a significant role in monitoring muscular tension from the demands of exercise, sport and daily lifestyle. Tension itself builds within our muscular framework from the gravitational forces placed on our body, whether through physical activity or a stationary position such as sitting down operating a computer. Many people are unaware of this latent build up of tension occurring over years like a silent time bomb.

In some cases symptoms of pain arise out of nowhere causing tension, muscle weakness, a limited range of movement and even reduced athletic performance. Whichever the case, it is recommended that regular monthly muscular-skeletal check-ups and adjustments be made by a certified physical therapist or osteopath to help manage ones musculoskeletal framework, especially when exercising or playing sport on a regular basis.

In the meantime, PMA serves as a valuable way for athletes to pinpoint muscular tension throughout the body. The term 'Passive' refers to muscles being tested without function or activity, generally in a lying position using a muscle gauge and release tool such as the Muscle Mate®. Emulating a clenched fist often used by an Osteopath to gauge and release muscular tension areas when working on their clients, the Muscle Mate can be used on the following areas to gauge, assess and help release muscular tension allowing you to communicate with your body. Below are a series of PMA exercises using the Muscle Mate:

Passive Muscle Assessment (PMA) with a trigger point release tool, such as the Muscle Mate:

- Always place Muscle Mate on muscle, never on bone
- Position under muscle and gently add pressure with bodyweight
- Hold position without pain for 5-30 seconds; gauge and release
- Relocate body position using small increments around area specified

Target Areas

Gluteal Region

Description:

Lie on back and roll legs to the side. Place Muscle Mate under upper portion of gluteal (butt) region. Roll legs back over to increase pressure and help release any tension. Using small incremental movements, work around whole gluteal region on left and right sides to help gauge and release muscular tension.

THE BODY COACH

Description:

Sit up with hands behind the back and roll legs to the side. Place Muscle Mate under mid buttock region and roll legs back over to increase load. Using small incremental movements, work around whole gluteal region on left and right sides to gauge and release tension.

Description:

Place Muscle Mate on floor with knob upwards. Position body on Muscle Mate between spine and shoulder blade on muscle (never bone). Roll body back across to feel pressure. Release and relocate by moving body. Work up and around shoulder blade on both sides to gauge and release tension. Extend arm overhead or raise hips to increase load on muscle group.

THE BODY COACH

4

Description:

Place Muscle Mate on floor with knob upwards. Position Muscle Mate on erector spinae muscle. Gently pull knee in towards chest to increase pressure. Release and relocate by moving body. Work up spinal muscles on left and right sides to gauge and release tension.

5 Calf and Forearm Regions

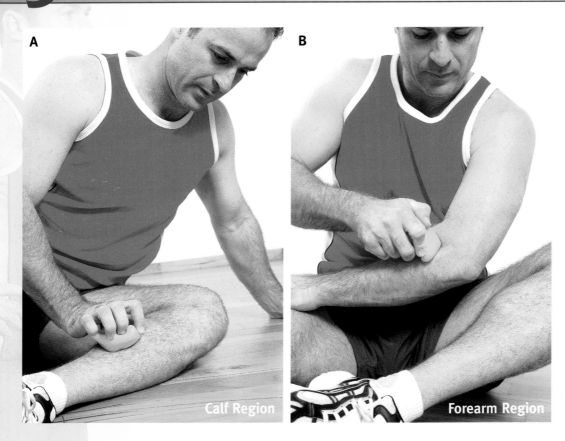

A

B

Calf Region

Forearm Region

5A. Calf Region

Using large knob, gently push Muscle Mate into calf region to gauge muscular tension. Release and relocate along calf region. Perform on left and right leg.

5B. Forearm Region

Using small knobs, gently push Muscle Mate into forearm region to gauge muscular tension. Release and relocate. Perform on left and right arm. Good for reducing tennis elbow or golfers wrist

For more information on the Muscle Mate® visit:
www.thebodycoach.com

Troubleshooting

On the following chart shade in areas of the body that may bring stress, muscular tension or restriction as found in Chapters 2 and 3. Refer to each chapter for appropriate stretches for these areas. If pain or tension has been a constant annoying aspect in your life each day, it is recommended to see a physical therapist for musculoskeletal assessment and treatment.

Chapter 4

Dynamic Warm-up – Stretching on the Move

A Dynamic Warm-up is designed to increase joint range of motion whilst stretching on the move. It involves a series of exercises of low to moderate intensity used to increase the body's core temperature and flexibility aiming to prepare the body for more demanding tasks ahead. The following exercises are performed at a slow to moderate pace to help and release muscular tension. Additional static stretches are used to release any further tension. A Dynamic Warm-up is a great way to start and finish a training session.

Perform dynamic warm-up exercises up and down preferred grid or set distance (ie. 10–20m) or stationary carry out the following drills:

Marching Forwards – Elbow to Knee

Cross elbow to opposite knee

Repeat action moving forward

Emphasis

- Promote high knee action and spine mobility

Description

- Start with arms flexed and fists at chin height
- March forwards raising one knee high
- Cross opposite elbow to opposite knee whilst marching forwards
- Look forward with chest held tall and head in neutral position
- Raise forward thigh up above parallel
- Cross forearm across body keeping torso upright
- Maintain focus and good body alignment whilst moving forwards
- Repeat movement on opposite leg as you move forwards

THE BODY COACH

Raise tall

Step wide

Emphasis

- Hip and leg strength, body alignment and stability.

Description

- Stand tall with hands on waist and feet together
- Step wide laterally (to the side) into half-squat position
- Perform continuous lateral movement cycle by stepping sideways again bringing feet together
- Complete length of grid leading with one leg and repeat leading with the opposite
- Maintain good body alignment – line from ear through shoulder, knee and ankle (lateral view) when performing squat action – avoid leaning forwards
- Maintain even balance between both legs

Raise tall with hands on hip

Lunge forwards

Emphasis

- Hip, foot and leg balance, alignment and co-ordination.

Description

- Stand tall with hands on hips
- Lunge forward and lower rear knee towards ground
- Continue forward lunge motion repeating action with opposite leg
- Maintain square hips at all times – avoid sagging or dropping
- Keep knee alignment over middle toes and sustain solid foot arch to avoid rolling knees inwards
- Look forward with chest held tall and head in neutral position
- Sustain deep breathing rhythm – breath-in as you lower and breath-out as you raise

THE BODY COACH

Legs apart

Step across, recover then step behind

Emphasis

- Increase hip range of motion and timing in lateral movement

Description

- Stand tall, feet together and hands on waist in a lateral (sideways) position to movement direction
- The rear foot crosses behind the body in a forward motion, then recover stepping across with feet wide and then crossing in front
- Maintain cycle along the length of the grid or set distance
- Repeat action in opposite direction with new lead foot
- Work off the balls of the feet as you transfer weight laterally and across, behind then in front of the body
- Start slowly and build up tempo
- Keep shoulders and arms square and parallel whilst body and hips rotate under you – avoid over twisting the upper body

Starting Position

Swing leg across body

Starting Position

- Stand behind chair with hands resting on back of chair for support

Action

- Raise up onto toes and take one leg forward
- Cross leg in front of body
- Keep toes of forward leg pulled back towards shin
- Brace abdominal muscles and hold good body position
- Swing leg out to side and back in a controlled manner with heel as the highest point
- Maintain deep breathing pattern
- Repeat movement on opposite leg

Note: *This exercise is performed only after thorough warm-up*

Chapter 5

Quadriceps and Anterior Hip Muscles

The Quadriceps is a large muscle having four bodies – rectus femoris, vastus lateralis, vastus medialis and vastus intermedius – which act together to extend the knee. The anterior hip muscles are stretched when the angle between the anterior and posterior surfaces of the thigh flex or extend.

THE BODY COACH

Rear View

Front View

Starting Position

- Stand tall with hands on waist.

Action

- Bend one leg, at the knee, up behind the body and grab the foot with the same hand and gently pull heel to buttocks
- Make sure the bent knee is kept in line with the opposite leg to reduce arching of the back and maximise stretch on bent front thigh
- Brace abdominal muscles and focus eyes on one point to maintain balance
- Use a chair or wall for support with the opposite hand, if necessary
- Hold stretch for up to 15 seconds or more
- Maintain deep breathing pattern
- Repeat stretch on opposite leg

Rear View

Side View

Starting Position

- Stand tall with hands on hips

Action

- Bend one leg, at the knee, up behind the body and grab the foot with the opposite hand and gently pull heel to buttocks
- Make sure the bent knee is kept in line with the opposite leg to reduce arching of the back and maximise stretch on bent front thigh.
- Brace abdominal muscles and focus eyes on one point to maintain balance
- Use a chair or wall for support with the opposite hand, if necessary
- Hold stretch for up to 15 seconds or more
- Maintain deep breathing pattern
- Repeat stretch on opposite leg

Starting Position

- Lie on side of body and use lower arm for support

Action

- Bend upper leg and grab foot with upper arm
- Gently pull heel to buttocks
- To reduce stress on lower back, brace abdominal muscles
- Make sure the bent leg is kept in line with the lower leg to reduce arching of the back and maximise stretch on bent front thigh
- Hold stretch for up to 15 seconds or more
- Maintain deep breathing pattern
- Repeat stretch on opposite leg

Starting Position

Tilt pelvis upwards and back

Starting Position

- Kneel in lunge position with rear knee on ground. Drop hip and lean chest slightly forward with hands on hip or front leg for support whilst rear leg bends back to 70–80 degree angle. (**Note:** hands placed on stomach and back to demonstrate body position and pelvic tilt)

Action

- Bracing abdominal muscles, tilt pelvis upwards and back and lock rear leg at 90–degree angle – no further
- Stretch is felt on front of rear thigh
- Keep chest cavity high and force rear leg forward without movement to stretch thigh
- Hold stretch for up to 15 seconds or more
- Maintain deep breathing pattern
- Repeat stretch on opposite leg

Starting Position

- Kneel in lunge position with rear knee on ground, toes pointed and hands resting on front thigh

Action

- Brace abdominal muscles to keep pelvis square
- Gently lean forward keeping, chest high, hands on thigh and body upright
- Hold stretch for up to 15 seconds or more
- Maintain deep breathing pattern
- Repeat stretch on opposite leg

Note: *See Exercise 47 for additional upper body stretch*

Supported Hip Flexors

Starting Position

- Kneel in lunge position with rear knee on ground (on folded towel, if necessary) and weight supported with hand on chair

Action

- Lift rear foot off ground and grab with hand of same leg
- Gently pull heel towards buttock
- Brace abdominal muscles, keep chest high and torso upright
- Hold stretch for up to 15 seconds or more
- Maintain deep breathing pattern
- Repeat stretch on opposite leg

Note: *If a partner is available, they may raise the rear leg whilst you support both hands on front thigh using exercise 5 position*

Starting Position

Action – lift rear knee

Starting Position

- Kneel in lunge position with rear knee on ground, resting on rear toes and hands resting on front thigh

Action

- Brace abdominal muscles to keep pelvis square
- Gently lean forward keeping, chest high, hands on thigh and body upright
- In extended position raise rear knee off ground
- Hold stretch for up to 15 seconds or more
- Maintain deep breathing pattern
- Repeat stretch on opposite leg

Chapter 6
Hamstrings

The hamstrings are a group of three posterior muscles working together to flex the knee and extend the thigh. The primary actions of the hamstrings are extension of the thigh and flexion of the knee.

Supported Hamstrings Stretch – Sitting

Raise on finger tips and lengthen spine

Keep spine long and gently lean forward

Starting Position

- Sit on ground with legs extended forwards and hands resting behind the body (on fingertips) with arms straight

Action

- Place one foot on top of the other
- Placing body weight on hands raise buttocks off ground briefly and lengthen spine
- Lower body and keep spine (torso) long
- Keeping arms and back straight, gently lean forward for stretch – avoiding any arching of back
- Hold stretch for up to 15 seconds or more
- Maintain deep breathing pattern
- Repeat stretch with opposite leg on top

THE BODY COACH

Starting Position

Straighten forward leg

Starting Position

- Kneel in lunge position with rear knee on ground, resting on rear toes and hands resting on front thigh

Action

- Sit back and straighten forward leg, keeping toes upright and towards shin
- Brace abdominal muscles to keep pelvis square and back straight
- Gently lean upper body forward keeping weight on hands on thighs at all times and back straight
- Keep front toes back towards shins to ensure effective stretch
- Hold stretch for up to 15 seconds or more
- Maintain deep breathing pattern
- Repeat stretch on opposite leg

Supported Hamstrings Stretch – Standing

Starting Position

- Stand tall with one leg forward

Action

- Lift front toes and rest front foot on heel
- Brace abdominal muscles and keep back straight
- Gently lean forward and place both hands on front thigh above the knee to reduce any stress on lower back
- Keep toes back towards shins to ensure effective stretch
- Hold stretch for up to 15 seconds or more
- Maintain deep breathing pattern
- Repeat stretch on opposite leg

Starting Position

- Stand tall and cross one leg forward of the other

Action

- Brace abdominal muscles to keep pelvis square and back straight
- Lean slightly forward and place hands on thigh above knee to support the lower back
- Bending arms slightly allow the weight of upper body to lower the body forward and stretch – keeping the legs straight
- Hold stretch for up to 15 seconds or more
- Maintain deep breathing pattern
- Repeat stretch with opposite leg forward

Lying Hamstrings Stretch – Bent Leg

Starting Position

Action – straighten leg

Starting Position

- Lie on your back with legs extended

Action

- Bend one knee towards chest
- Place both hands behind knee for support – keeping the leg slightly bent
- Gently straighten leg keeping the hands behind the knees
- Hold stretch for up to 15 seconds or more
- Maintain deep breathing pattern
- Repeat stretch with opposite leg

Note: *If unable to straighten raised leg, bend lower supporting leg and repeat action*

Starting Position

- Lie on your back with legs extended

Action

- Lift one leg from the hip and grasp calf region with both hands
- Keeping the leg straight, gently pull leg towards the upper body
- Ensure the extended leg remains on the ground
- Raise the head and shoulders off the ground
- Hold stretch for up to 15 seconds or more
- Maintain deep breathing pattern
- Repeat stretch with opposite leg

Lying Hamstring Stretch – with Towel

Starting Position

- Lie on back, bend one knee and place towel around raised foot

Action

- Holding towel with both hands, slowly straighten leg into air
- Keep a solid grip with toes pulled back towards shins
- Once straight gently pull leg towards upper body
- Ensure the extended (lower) leg remains on the ground
- Hold stretch for up to 15 seconds or more
- Maintain deep breathing pattern
- Repeat stretch with opposite leg

THE BODY COACH

Starting Position

- Stand one step away from front of chair

Action

- Raise one leg up onto chair or bench and straighten leg
- Place hands on thigh above knee to support lower back
- Turn the rear foot of supporting leg directly forward
- Flex toes towards shin of raised leg
- Brace abdominal muscles; keep back straight and pelvis square
- Gently lean forward for stretch
- Hold stretch for up to 15 seconds or more
- Maintain deep breathing pattern
- Repeat stretch on opposite leg

Action A

Action B

Turn foot slightly outwards

Turn foot slightly inwards

Starting Position

- Stand one step away from front of chair

Action

- Raise one leg up onto chair or bench and straighten leg
- Place hands on thigh above knee to support lower back
- Turn the rear foot of supporting leg directly forward
- Flex toes towards shin of raised leg and:
  A: Turn raised foot **outwards** to stretch the lateral hamstring
  B: Turn raised foot **inwards** to stretch medial hamstring
- Brace abdominal muscles; keep back straight and pelvis square
- Gently lean forward for stretch
- Hold stretch for up to 15 seconds or more
- Maintain deep breathing pattern
- Repeat stretch on opposite leg

Chapter 7

Lower Limb

The major muscles of the lower limb consist of two distinct parts called the gastrocnemius (or calf) and soleus that merge with the Achilles tendon and act on movements of the ankle. Dorsiflexion at the ankle stretches the soleus. To stretch the calf, you must add extension of the knee.

THE BODY COACH

Calf Stretch

Starting Position

- Stand facing wall in a forward lunge position

Action

- Bend forward leg and place hands against wall
- Push hips forward whilst keeping the rear leg straight and pushing the heel of the rear leg into the ground for stretch
- Hold stretch for up to 15 seconds or more
- Maintain deep breathing pattern
- Repeat stretch on opposite leg

Calf Stretch - off Raised Step

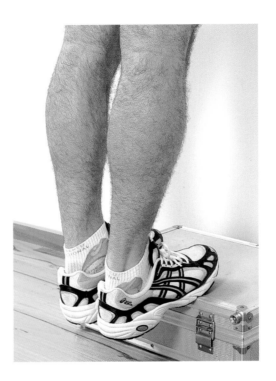

Starting Position

- Stand on ball of foot on edge of step

Action

- Lean body slightly forward as you lower heels off step
- Hold onto wall or hand support
- Hold stretch for up to 15 seconds or more
- Maintain deep breathing pattern

Variation
- Single leg stretch – resting one foot behind the other off the edge of step for stretch

THE BODY COACH

Starting Position

- Raise into front support position on hands and feet

Action

- Keep eye line forwards over fingernails and abdominal muscles braced
- Lift one leg and place toes behind heel of lower leg
- Gently lower hips towards ground keeping heel of lower leg pushing into ground for stretch
- Hold stretch for up to 15 seconds or more
- Maintain deep breathing pattern
- Repeat on opposite leg

Soleus Stretch – Standing

Starting Position

- Stand with one foot forward and hands on hips

Action

- Simultaneously bend forward and rear leg
- Keep body centred and torso upright
- Keep rear heel pushed into ground for stretch
- Hold stretch for up to 15 seconds or more
- Maintain deep breathing pattern
- Repeat stretch on opposite leg

Starting Position

- Kneel on ground on one leg

Action

- Align foot with knee
- Lean forward and place chest on thigh and hands on ground
- Keep heel of forward foot pushed into ground for stretch
- Hold stretch for up to 15 seconds or more
- Maintain deep breathing pattern
- Repeat stretch on opposite leg

Chapter 8
Adductors
(groin)

The adductors group lies on the internal side of the thigh. Adduction of the hip is the movement of the lower limb toward the midline of the body. This movement is produced primarily by five muscles – adductor longus, adductor brevis and adductor magnus and assisted by the pectineus and gracilis muscles.

Adductors – Sitting

Starting Position

Action

Starting Position

- Sit on floor with soles of feet together

Action

- Grasp your ankles with your hands and rest forearms along lower leg, resting elbows against knees
- Gently push knees down towards ground using elbows
- Keep torso upright
- Hold stretch for up to 15 seconds or more
- Maintain deep breathing pattern

Starting Position

- Stand tall with feet one and a half shoulder-widths apart

Action

- Lower body into a squat position by bending knees and place elbows inside the leg and against knees
- Upper body is bent slightly forward to counteract body balance
- Gently push knees out to side with elbows
- Hold stretch for up to 10 seconds
- Maintain deep breathing pattern

Note: *Avoid this exercise if you have knee or lower back pain or tension*

Starting Position

- Lie sideways (parallel) against wall with body extended along wall

Action

- Raise both legs vertical
- Twist hips and body away from wall at 90-degree angle
- This action allow buttocks to stay close to wall
- Simultaneously open legs and gently lower legs out to side
- Hold stretch for up to 15 seconds or more
- Maintain deep breathing pattern

Action

Advanced version

Starting Position

- Sit on floor with legs apart

Action

- Brace abdominal muscles and keep torso upright
- Keep toes pointing upwards
- Grasp toes with hands for support of lower back
- Gently lean torso forwards keeping back flat – avoiding rounding of back or shoulders
- Hold stretch for up to 15 seconds or more
- Maintain deep breathing pattern

Advanced Version

- With legs wide, torso long and back flat, place hands behind the body with arms straight – resting on finger tips
- Keeping toes pointed upwards and chest tall gently lean forwards using straight arms to assist stretch
- Hold stretch for up to 15 seconds or more
- Maintain deep breathing pattern

Note: *See Exercise 40 for additional stretch*

Starting Position

- Place hands on floor and spread legs wide keeping chest parallel to ground

Action

- Point toes forwards 45-degrees and roll onto inside of foot to increase stretch angle
- Keep weight on hands to avoid overloading adductors
- Hold stretch for up to 15 seconds or more
- Maintain deep breathing pattern

Note: *See Exercise 40 for increasing Iliopsoas flexibility*

Chapter 9

Gluteal (buttock)

and

Hip Region

The antagonists of the adductors, the abductors can be found on the lateral surface of the pelvis. This muscle group is covered by the gluteus maximus – the large superficial muscle that provides the bulk of the buttocks. Located under the gluteus maximus is a group of external rotators. The gluteal muscle is the major hip extensor, and also acts in lateral rotation.

THE BODY COACH

Starting Position

- Sit upright on floor with both legs extended

Action

- Flex one leg and cross it over the other leg and place foot on ground.
- Using the opposite arm support the knee of the bent leg with your hand
- Gently turn shoulders towards opposite knee for stretch
- The other hand rests behind the body for support
- Keep buttocks on ground with chest high and back upright
- Hold stretch for up to 15 seconds or more
- Maintain deep breathing pattern
- Repeat stretch on opposite leg

Variation

- Lie on back, bend one knee and cross foot over opposite leg
- Grab knee of bent leg and pull towards chest

Starting Position

- Sit upright on floor with both legs extended

Action

- Bend one knee and grab ankle with both hands
- Rest forearm on same side of leg across shin with elbow against knee
- Gently push elbow against knee and bring foot upwards with hands
- Hold stretch for up to 15 seconds or more
- Keep upper body upright
- Maintain deep breathing pattern
- Repeat stretch on opposite leg

THE BODY COACH

Starting Position

- Lie on back, bend one knee and place towel around raised foot

Action

- Hold towel with both hands and place elbow against knee of bent leg
- With forearm resting against thigh, gently pull foot downwards in small arch towards ground
- Ensure the extended leg remains on the ground
- Hold stretch for up to 15 seconds or more
- Maintain deep breathing pattern
- Repeat stretch with opposite leg

Starting Position

- Lie on back with knees bent

Action

- Lift one leg and place foot on opposite knee
- Lift both feet off ground
- Simultaneously extend arm of raised leg in-between legs and the other to the outside of leg and grab knee
- Gently pull legs towards body
- Raise head and shoulders off the ground to increase stretch
- Hold stretch for up to 15 seconds or more
- Maintain deep breathing pattern
- Repeat stretch with opposite leg

Starting Position

- Lie on back with knees bent facing a wall

Action

- Lift one leg and place foot against wall with leg at 90-degrees
- Bend the opposite leg and rest foot across opposite knee
- Place hand on knee and gently push knee towards wall for stretch
- Brace abdominal muscles and keep back flat to avoid movement
- Hold stretch for up to 15 seconds or more
- Maintain deep breathing pattern
- Repeat stretch with opposite leg

Note: *See Chapter 11 for additional stretches for this region*

Starting Position

- Lie on back with knees bent and arms out to the side

Action

- Lift one leg and rest foot across opposite knee
- Lower legs to side of raised knee and turn head across to opposite side for stretch
- Hold stretch for up to 15 seconds or more
- Maintain deep breathing pattern
- Repeat stretch with opposite leg

Chapter 10
Hip, Pelvic and Lumbar Regions

The pelvic girdle and their muscle attachments support the trunk and also serves as an abutment for the lower extremities and a base for their mobility. Keeping the muscles of the hip, pelvic and lumbar regions pliable, stable and strong provides an excellent platform for protecting the lower back region and reducing the risk of injury.

Starting Position

- Lie on back on ground with legs extended and arms by your side

Action

- Lift one leg and bend knee towards chest
- Grip knee with both hands and gently pull towards chest for stretch
- Brace abdominal muscles and keep torso long
- Ensure the extended leg remains on the ground with foot upright
- Hold stretch for up to 15 seconds or more
- Maintain deep breathing pattern
- Repeat stretch with opposite leg

Knees to chest

Raise head and shoulders

Starting Position

- Lie on back on ground with legs extended and arms by your side

Action

- Lift both legs and bend knees towards chest
- Grip knees with both hands and gently pull towards chest for stretch – keep legs close together
- Brace abdominal muscles and keep torso long
- For additional stretch to spine raise head and shoulders off ground towards knees
- Hold stretch for up to 15 seconds or more
- Maintain deep breathing pattern

THE BODY COACH

Starting Position

- Kneel on ground on shins and sit back on legs

Action

- Gently lean forward with torso lowering over thighs
- Extend arms forward of the body
- Keep buttocks down on top of heels
- Hold stretch for up to 15 seconds or more
- Maintain deep breathing pattern

Note: *This exercise also stretches your shoulders, arms and back muscles including the latissimus dorsi.*

Starting Position

- Lie on ground on stomach with legs extended

Action

- Place rolled towel (or Lumbatube™) under pelvic region
- Place hands under chin and rest head to side
- Brace abdominal muscles and maintain deep breathing pattern
- Hold stretch for up to 15 seconds or more

Starting Position

- Stand in front of fitness ball

Action

- Kneel down and lie across fitness ball on stomach
- Support body through hands and feet either side of fitness ball
- Feel centred and allow body to sink into the ball
- Maintain deep breathing pattern
- Hold stretch for up to 15 seconds or more

Back Extension – Elbows

Starting Position

- Lie on stomach with arms bent and clench fists placed directly under chin for head to rest upon

Action

- Gently brace the abdominal muscles and hold
- Slowly raise head and chest from ground, keeping spine long
- Maintain deep breathing pattern
- Avoid overarching lower back. No pain or tension should be present
- Hold stretch for up to 15 seconds, then lower

Note: *Follow this stretch with Exercise 34 to release any tension*

THE BODY COACH

Starting Position

- Lie on stomach with arms bent and palms resting on the ground beside your shoulders

Action

- Gently brace the abdominal muscles and hold
- Slowly raise head and chest from ground, keeping spine long
- Extend arms and keep weight on palms of hand
- Maintain deep breathing pattern
- Avoid overarching lower back. No pain or tension should be present
- Hold stretch for up to 15 seconds, then lower

* This exercise is for advanced exercisers only

Note: *Follow this stretch with Exercise 34 to release any tension*

40 Iliopsoas*

Variation 1

Variation 2

Starting Position

- Spread legs wide and lean forward and place both hands on the ground

Action – Variation 1

- Gently brace the abdominal muscles and hold
- Turn feet out and rest on instep of both feet on ground
- Maintain weight on hands and keep arms extended
- Slowly lower hips to ground keeping head raised and spine long
- No pain or tension should be present
- Maintain deep breathing pattern
- Hold stretch for up to 15 seconds

Action – Variation 2

- Turn to one side and raise onto heel of front foot and toes of back foot and lower hip to ground
- Maintain weight on hands and keep arms extended
- Hold stretch for up to 15 seconds
- Maintain deep breathing pattern
- Repeat stretch on opposite side

* This exercise is for advanced exercisers only – ie. martial artists

Chapter 11

Iliotibial Band (ITB) and Sacroiliac Joint

The superficial potion of the gluteus maximus, and tensor fascia latae (TFL), insert onto the iliotibial (ITB) tract from opposite directions and play an important role as stabilizers of the hip and knee joints during standing and walking. The hip bones are connected to the sacrum through the sacroiliac joints and pubic bone. The sacrum and sacroiliac joint serves as a strong foundation for the pelvic girdle.

THE BODY COACH

Standing ITB Stretch

Starting Position

- Stand with legs crossed, hands on hips

Action

- Gently brace the abdominal muscles and hold
- With right leg crossed behind left push hips across to right side
- Keeping rear leg straight, lean torso and head in opposite direction for counterbalance – let the hip do the work
- Maintain deep breathing pattern
- Hold stretch for up to 15 seconds or more
- Repeat movement with left leg crossed behind body

Kneeling ITB Stretch

Starting Position

- Kneel on ground in forward lunge position with rear knee on ground and hand of rear knee on chair for support

Action

- Gently lower hip sideways towards chair for stretch
- Keep weight on hand (on chair) for support and torso long
- Maintain deep breathing pattern
- Hold stretch for up to 15 seconds or more
- Repeat movement on opposite side

THE BODY COACH

Starting Position

- Stand in front of chair

Action

- Raise one leg and place foot up onto chair
- Bend leg and rest foot on its outside – toes pointing forward
- Place both hands on inside of bent knee
- Rear foot is pointing forwards
- Brace abdominal muscles and keeping torso long
- Gently lean forward over foot for stretch
- Maintain deep breathing pattern
- Hold stretch for up to 15 seconds or more
- Repeat movement on opposite leg

Starting Position

- Kneel on ground on both knees and rest body forwards on forearms

Action

- Brace abdominal muscles and hold, keeping back flat
- Keeping leg straight, cross right leg behind body to left side
- Ensure upper body remains square
- Maintain deep breathing pattern
- Hold stretch for up to 15 seconds or more
- Repeat movement with left leg

Starting Position

Gently lean forward

Starting Position

- Stand in front of table or bench and raise one leg

Action

- Raise and bend one leg in front of body and up onto table
- Keep thigh and knee pointing forwards from body
- Rest on foot on table inline with opposite shoulder
- Place hands forwards of the body on the table
- Rear foot is pointing forwards
- Square up shoulders over forward leg
- Gently lower forwards for stretch
- Hold stretch for up to 15 seconds or more
- Repeat movement on opposite leg

Note: *Avoid exercise if you suffer knee pain*

Chapter 12

Upper Body Region – Back, Shoulders, Chest and Arms

Collectively the muscles of the upper body region act on the trunk, shoulder girdle, spine and neck to place them in a suitable position for more efficient movements of the upper extremity

Standing Side Reach

Starting Position

- Stand tall with hands on hips and feet shoulder width apart

Action

- Brace abdominal muscles and extend one-arm above the head
- Lean raised arm across to opposite side for stretch
- Avoid leaning forwards or backwards when leaning to the side
- Reach for sky with raised arm whilst bending across to keep spine long
- Maintain deep breathing pattern
- Hold stretch for up to 15 seconds or more
- Repeat movement on opposite side

Variation
- Stand next to pole and grasp with opposite hand overhead. Lean hips away from pole for side stretch

THE BODY COACH

Starting Position

- Kneel in lunge position with legs at 90-degrees

Action

- Gently lean forward and place forearm across forward leg
- Raise rear arm into the air
- Brace abdominal muscles to keep pelvis square
- Gently bend legs and lean forward
- Extend raised arm (and shoulder) slightly back and across for stretch
- Hold stretch for up to 15 seconds or more
- Maintain deep breathing pattern
- Repeat stretch on opposite side

Mid Back Squeeze

Starting Position

- Stand tall with arms resting by your side

Action

- Brace abdominal muscles and hold
- Lift chest and turn palms forwards with thumbs rotating outwards
- Bring shoulder blades together
- Avoid arching lower back
- Maintain deep breathing pattern
- Hold stretch for up to 15 seconds or more

THE BODY COACH

Starting Position

- Stand arms length from wall

Action

- Extend arms forward and place hands on wall
- Bend knees and hip and lower upper body forwards
- Maintain hand placement as the body lowers for stretch
- Keep legs upright and torso parallel to ground with gentle arch through back
- Hold stretch for up to 15 seconds or more
- Maintain deep breathing pattern

Variation 1

Variation 2

Starting Position

- Stand tall with arms resting by your side

Action – Variation 1

- Lean head to right side and place fingers of right hand on head
- Extend left arm out to the side and reach down for stretch
- Maintain deep breathing pattern
- Hold stretch for up to 15 seconds
- Repeat opposite side

Action – Variation 2

- Lean head to right side
- Extend left arm behind body and grip with right hand for stretch
- Maintain deep breathing pattern
- Hold stretch for up to 15 seconds
- Repeat opposite side

Chest Stretch

Starting Position

- Stand between doorframe

Action

- Raise arms, bend at 90-degrees and rest forearms along doorframe
- Stand with one foot forward of the other
- Brace abdominal muscles
- Gently lean chest and body weight forwards for stretch
- Maintain deep breathing pattern
- Hold stretch for up to 15 seconds or more

Note: *This stretch can also be performed in the corner of two walls*

Neck Isometrics (static stretch)

Variation 1

Variation 2

Starting Position

- Stand with hands on waist

Action – Variation 1

- Place one hand on side of head
- Simultaneously push hand inwards and head outwards for static stretch
- Hold stretch for up to 15 seconds
- Maintain deep breathing pattern
- Repeat opposite side

Action – Variation 2

- Place one hand on front of head
- Simultaneously push hand inwards and head outwards for static stretch
- Hold stretch for up to 15 seconds
- Maintain deep breathing pattern

Extend and Raise Arms

Variation 1

Extend arms forward

Variation 2

Raise arms overhead

Starting Position
- Stand tall with arms by side

Action – Variation 1
- Interlock fingers and raise arms parallel to ground push palms outwards
- Hold stretch for up to 15 seconds or more
- Maintain deep breathing pattern

Action – Variation 2
- Brace abdominal muscles
- Raise arms up overhead and reach for sky
- Reach up through shoulders
- Hold stretch for up to 15 seconds or more
- Maintain deep breathing pattern

Lateral Shoulder Cross-over

Starting Position

- Stand tall with arms by side

Action

- Raise one arm to shoulder height
- Flex arm across to opposite shoulder
- Grasp raised elbow with opposite forearm and pull inwards for stretch
- Hold stretch for up to 15 seconds or more
- Maintain deep breathing pattern
- Repeat opposite side

THE BODY COACH

Arm behind head

Test – grasp hands

Starting Position
- Stand tall with arms by side

Action
- Extend one arm upwards overhead
- Bend elbow and lower behind head
- Grasp elbow with opposite hand and gently pull downwards for stretch
- Hold stretch for up to 15 seconds or more
- Maintain deep breathing pattern
- Repeat opposite side

Test
- One test of upper body flexibility is the ability to grasp both hands behind the body (as shown above). Repeat test on both sides.

Starting Position

- Stand tall with arms by side

Action

- Extend one arm forwards with palm facing upwards
- Grasp fingers with opposite hand on top of palm
- Bend wrist and gently pull fingers downwards with opposite hand for stretch
- Hold stretch for up to 15 seconds or more
- Maintain deep breathing pattern
- Repeat opposite side

THE BODY COACH

Starting Position

- Kneel on ground on all fours – hands and knees

Action

- With palms resting on ground, rotate thumbs outwards – forearms now facing forwards
- Keep palms flat as you lean back to stretch forearms
- Hold stretch for up to 15 seconds or more
- Maintain deep breathing pattern

Single Arm Chest Stretch

Variation 1

Variation 2

Starting Position

- Stand next to wall

Action – Variation 1

- Raise one arm and bend at 90-degrees
- Rest forearm and palm against wall with upper arm parallel to ground
- Step forward keeping arm in same position for stretch
- Repeat opposite arm

Action – Variation 2

- Face wall and raise one arm up and parallel to ground
- Rest forearm and palm against wall in extended position
- Turn feet and shoulders away from wall for stretch without losing arm contact
- Maintain deep breathing pattern
- Hold stretch for up to 15 seconds or more
- Repeat stretch on opposite arm

Starting Position

- Kneel on ground on shins and sit back on legs

Action

- Extend one arm forward of the body and the other bent
- Brace abdominal muscles and hold keeping hips square
- Gently lean forward with extended arms and press down slightly with palms for stretch
- Keep buttocks down on top of heels
- Hold stretch for up to 15 seconds or more
- Maintain deep breathing pattern
- Repeat stretch with opposite arm

Note: *Also see Exercise 35 for double arm variation*

Starting Position

- Lie on back on ground

Action

- Extend arms overhead and point toes
- Brace abdominal muscles and hold
- Extend arms and feet in opposite directions away from centre of body for stretch
- Avoid arching of lower back
- Hold stretch for up to 15 seconds or more
- Maintain deep breathing pattern

Chapter 13

General
Stretching
Routines

This series of sample stretching routines is designed for general everyday use. They can be added to or varied depending on the individual's strengths and weaknesses in range of motion and the requirements of training, sport or daily lifestyle. A stretching routine can vary from performing a single stretch regularly throughout the day or a routine of 10-20 minutes or more. Static stretching is preferable, mainly because the muscles are more relaxed. Take the time to relax and enjoy each stretch rather than rushing in an effort to get them over and done with.

Below are a series of sample stretching routines. Refer to chapters for descriptions of each stretching exercise.

Please note: These routines do not replace proper medical advice. If you have been inactive or sedentary for some time, suffered an injury recently or in the past seek medical advice before starting any exercise program or stretching routine.

Passive Muscle Assessment (PMA): Muscle Mate® Summary

To help assess and identify muscular 'hot spots' holding tension, perform a PMA assessment on the following areas and seek appropriate medical advice if pain arises, before starting or continuing with exercises or physical activity.

- Always place Muscle Mate® on muscle, never on bone
- Position under muscle and gently add pressure with bodyweight
- Hold position without pain for 5-30 seconds; gauge and release
- Relocate body position using small increments around area specified
- See Chapter 3 for more details

Gluteal Region p.26

Piriformis p.27

Shoulder Girdle p.28

Lower Back p.29

Calf Region p.30

Forearm Region p.30

Reducing Lower Back Tension

- Always make sure your muscles are warmed-up before you stretch
- Hold each stretch for up to 15 seconds or longer
- Hold the stretch in a comfortable position rather than strain or overstress the muscle – do not bounce.
- Perform Passive Muscle Assessment (PMA) prior to stretching

Standing thigh cross-over p.42

Kneeling pelvic tilt p.44

Raised leg hamstrings stretch p.57

Calf stretch p.61

Sacroiliac & ITB p.95

Kneeling side reach p.101

THE BODY COACH

Back extension – elbows p.88

Piriformis p.78

Lumbar rotation p.80

Note: *Also see Exercises 36 and 37 on pelvic release*

Pre-and-Post Work Stretching Routine

- Always make sure your muscles are warmed-up before you stretch
- Hold each stretch for up to 15 seconds or longer
- Hold the stretch in a comfortable position rather than strain or overstress the muscle – do not bounce.
- Perform Passive Muscle Assessment (PMA) prior to stretching

Standing thigh stretch p.41

Kneeling hip flexors p.45

Supported hamstring stretch – standing p.52

Calf stretch p.61

Standing side reach p.100

Neck and shoulders p.104

Back extension – elbows p.88

Reverse hip and thoracic rotation p.75

Piriformis p.78

Chest stretch p.105

Extend and raise p.107

Triceps p.109

3–Minute Office Stretching Routine

- Take three deep breaths
- Hold each stretch for up to 15 seconds or longer
- Hold the stretch in a comfortable position rather than strain
- Drink 8 glasses of water a day to keep hydrated
- Stretch regularly throughout the day

Interlock fingers and reach forward

Reach upwards with interlocked fingers

Knee to chest – left and right side

Hamstrings Stretch – left and right side

Thigh Stretch – left and right side

Side Stretch – left and right side

THE BODY COACH

Chapter 14

Sports Specific Stretching Routines

This series of sample stretching routines is designed for athletes in general. They can be added to or varied depending on the athlete's strengths and weaknesses and the requirements of training or sport. A stretching routine plays an important role in the management of muscular pliability and flexibility and maintaining joint range of motion. A static stretching routine after training or playing sport and in-between sessions should be performed on a regular basis along with massage and physical therapy treatment.

Below are a series of sample stretching routines. Refer to chapters throughout this book for descriptions of each stretching exercise. Before you get started, the muscles need to be warm, whether after a warm shower, light exercise or sport as this helps prepare the your body and bring a better response from the muscles being stretched.

Stretching Guidelines
- Warm-up prior to stretching
- Hold each stretch up to 15 seconds or longer
- Hold each stretch in a comfortable position, without pain
- Apply Passive Muscle Assessment (PMA) prior to stretching to gauge muscular tension

Please note: These routines do not replace proper medical advice. If you have been inactive or sedentary for some time, suffered an injury recently or in the past seek medical advice before starting any exercise program or stretching routine.

THE BODY COACH

General Sports Stretching Routine

Lateral Thigh Stretch p.43

Supported Hamstring Stretch p.50

Reverse Hip & Thoracic Rotation p.75

Piriformis p.78

Back extension – elbows p.88

Kneeling sacroiliac joint p.96

Kneeling Hip Flexors p.45

Extend and raise p.107

Standing side reach p.100

Chest stretch p.105

Triceps p.109

Calf stretch p.61

Ball Sports

Sports include: AFL, Basketball, Handball, Netball, Volleyball (see also running-specific stretches p. 136)

Gluteal Region (PMA) p.26

Piriformis p.78

Reverse Hip and Thoracic Rotation p.75

Supported Hamstring Stretch p.50

Back extension – elbows p.88

Shoulder Girdle (PMA) p.28

THE BODY COACH

Kneeling Side Reach p.101

Calf stretch p.61

**Raised Sacroiliac and ITB
Stretch p.97**

Single Arm Chest stretch p.112

Triceps p.109

Extend and Raise Arms p.107

Balance Sports

Sports include: Cycling, Ice-skating, Kite-boarding, Skate-boarding, Snow-Boarding, Snow-skiing, Surfing (also see swimming), Wakeboarding, Water-skiing and Windsurfing

Gluteal Region (PMA) p.26

Shoulder Girdle (PMA) p.28

Lower Back (PMA) p.29

Back extension – elbows p.88

Soleus Stretch p.65

Reverse Hip and Thoracic Rotation p.75

THE BODY COACH

Hamstrings p. 57

Sacroiliac & ITB p. 95

Standing Thigh p. 41

Single Arm Chest stretch p.112

Standing side reach p.100

Triceps p.109

Golf Specific

Back extension – elbows p.88

Gluteal Region (PMA) p.26

Shoulder Girdle (PMA) p.28

Reverse Hip and Thoracic Rotation p.75

THE BODY COACH

Spine Rotation p.18

Single Arm Chest stretch p.112

Mid-Back Arch p.103

Hamstrings p.57

Standing Thigh p.41

Calf stretch p.61

Triceps p. 109

Standing side reach p.100

Martial Arts

Sports include: Aikido, Judo, Karate, Kung Fu, Taekwondo

Adductors – Side splits p.72

Iliopsoas p.90

Lying Hamstrings p.55

Adductors – Legs Wide p.71

Front Splits p.21

Reverse Hip and Thoracic Rotation p.75

THE BODY COACH

Kneeling Pelvic tilt p.44

Kneeling Side Reach p.101

Dynamic Lateral leg Swings p.38

Single Arm Stretch p.112

Mid-Back Arch p.103

Neck and Shoulders p.104

Racquet and Bat Sports

Sports include: Badminton, Baseball, Cricket, Hockey, Lacrosse, Softball, Squash and Tennis – also see running

Forearm Region (PMA) p.30

Gluteal Region (PMA) p.26

Shoulder Girdle (PMA) p.28

Piriformis p.78

Back extension – elbows p.88

Kneeling sacroiliac joint p.96

THE BODY COACH

Kneeling Side Reach p.101

Hamstrings p.57

Calf Stretch p.61

Chest stretch p.105

Triceps p.109

Spine Rotation p.18

Running Specific

Sports include: AFL, Athletics, NFL, Rugby League, Rugby Union, Soccer

Gluteal Region (PMA) p.26

Piriformis p.78

Reverse Hip and Thoracic Rotation p.75

Piriformis (PMA) p.27

Iliopsoas p.90

Kneeling Pelvic tilt p.44

THE BODY COACH

Sacroiliac & ITB p.95

Hamstrings p.57

Dynamic Lateral leg Swings p.38

Chest stretch p.105

Kneeling Side Reach p.101

Calf Stretch p.61

Swimming Specific

Sports include: Diving, Surfing, Swimming, Water Polo

Gluteal Region (PMA) p.26

Piriformis p.78

Reverse Hip and Thoracic Rotation p.75

Piriformis (PMA) p.27

Iliopsoas p.90

Shoulder Girdle (PMA) p.28

THE BODY COACH

Kneeling Pelvic tilt p.44

Single Arm Stretch p.112

Spine Rotation p.18

Mid-Back Arch p.103

Kneeling Side Reach p.101

Extend and Raise Arms p.107

The Body Coach® – Products and Services

BOOK SERIES
The Body Coach® Book Series
- The Body Coach provides the latest cutting edge fitness training books written in a user-friendly format that is so advanced, that it's actually simple.

SEMINARS
The Body Coach® Keynotes and Seminars
- Corporate health and wellbeing keynote presentations
- Convention partner programs
- Seminars and Workshops
- Exclusive 5-star VIP Coaching – World-wide
- TV, Radio, interactive and Print Media Services

COURSES
The Body Coach® Programs and Courses
- Personal Training Certification Courses
- Continuing Education Courses (CEC)
- Licensed Group Fitness: Fastfeet®, Quickfeet®, Posturefit®, Swimstrength™, Kidstrength™
- Weight Loss Programs – Thigh Busters®, Belly Busters®, 3 Hour Rule®

PRODUCTS
Body Coach® Fitness Products and Brand Licensing
- Product Range – Speedhoop®, Spinal Unloading Block™, Muscle Mate®, Lumbatube™, Itibulator™, Rebound Medicine Ball™ & more...
- Product Education – Book and DVD Productions
- Product Brand Licensing opportunities

International Managing Agent
Saxton Speakers Bureau (Australia)
- Website: www.saxton.com.au
- Email: speakers@saxton.com.au
- Phone: (03) 9811 3500
  International: +61 3 9811 3500

www.thebodycoach.com

Stretching Index

Testing Flexibility and Range of Motion

1. Triceps 16
2. Groin 17
3. Wall Slide 17
4. Spine Rotation 18
5. Hamstrings and Balance 19
6. Adductors – Side Splits 20
7. Hamstrings – Front Splits 21
8. Squat Range of Motion 22

Passive Muscle Assessment

1. Gluteal Region 26
2. Piriformis 27
3. Shoulder Girdle 28
4. Lower Back 29
5A. Calf Region 30
5B. Forearm Region 30

Dynamic Warm-up – Stretching on the Move

1. Marching Elbow to Knee 34
2. Side Squat 35
3. Walking Lunges 36
4. Carioca 37
5. Dynamic Lateral Leg Swings 38

Quadriceps

Exercise 1 — Standing Thigh Stretch 41
Exercise 2 — Standing Thigh Cross-over 42
Exercise 3 — Lateral Thigh Stretch 43
Exercise 4 — Kneeling Pelvic Tilt 44
Exercise 5 — Kneeling Hip Flexors 45
Exercise 6 — Supporting Hip Flexors 46
Exercise 7 — Raised Hip Flexors 47

Hamstrings

Exercise 8 — Supported Hamstrings Stretch – Seated 50
Exercise 9 — Supported Hamstrings Stretch – Kneeling 51
Exercise 10 — Supported Hamstrings Stretch – Standing 52
Exercise 11 — Supported Cross-leg Hamstrings Stretch 53
Exercise 12 — Lying Hamstrings Stretch – Bent Leg 54
Exercise 13 — Lying Hamstrings Stretch – Straight Leg 55

Exercise 14 — Lying Hamstrings Stretch – Towel 56
Exercise 15 — Raised Leg Hamstrings Stretch 57
Exercise 16 — Raised Leg Hamstrings – Angles 58

Lower Limb
Exercise 17 — Calf Stretch .61
Exercise 18 — Calf Stretch – off Raised Step 62
Exercise 19 — Calf Stretch – Front Support 63
Exercise 20 — Soleus Stretch – Standing 64
Exercise 21 — Soleus Stretch – Kneeling 65

Adductors (groin)
Exercise 22 — Adductors – Sitting 68
Exercise 23 — Adductors – Squating 69
Exercise 24 — Adductors – Wall Lying 70
Exercise 25 — Adductors – Legs Wide (sitting) 71
Exercise 26 — Adductors – Side Splits 72

Gluteal (buttock) and Hip Region
Exercise 27 — Reverse Hip and Thoracic Rotation 75
Exercise 28 — Seated Buttock and Hip Stretch 76
Exercise 29 — Lying Buttock and Hip Stretch with Towel 77
Exercise 30 — Deep Gluteal Region – Piriformis 78
Exercise 31 — Deep Gluteal Region – Foot on Wall 79
Exercise 32 — Lumbar Rotation 80

Hip, Pelvic and Lumbar Regions
Exercise 33 — Single-Leg Hip Flexion 83
Exercise 34 — Knees to Chest .84
Exercise 35 — Forward Flexion .85
Exercise 36 — Pelvic Release – Lying on Ground 86
Exercise 37 — Pelvic Release – Lying on Fitness Ball 87
Exercise 38 — Back Extension – Elbows 88
Exercise 39 — Back Extension – Hands 89
Exercise 40 — Illiopsoas 90

Iliotibial Band (ITB)
Exercise 41 — Standing ITB Stretch 93
Exercise 42 — Kneeling ITB Stretch 94
Exercise 43 — Sacroiliac and ITB Stretch – Standing 95
Exercise 44 — Kneeling Sacroiliac Joint 96
Exercise 45 — Raised Sacroiliac and ITB 97

THE BODY COACH

Upper Body Region – Back and Shoulders

Exercise 46 — Standing Side Reach 100
Exercise 47 — Kneeling Side Reach 101
Exercise 48 — Mid-Back Squeeze 102
Exercise 49 — Mid Back Arch 103
Exercise 50 — Neck and Shoulders .104
Exercise 51 — Chest Stretch 105
Exercise 52 — Neck Isometrics (static) 106
Exercise 53 — Extend and Raise Arms 107
Exercise 54 — Lateral Shoulder Cross-over 108
Exercise 55 — Triceps Stretch 109
Exercise 56 — Wrist and Forearm Standing 110
Exercise 57 — Wrist and Forearm Kneeling 111
Exercise 58 — Single Arm Chest Stretch 112
Exercise 59 — Single Arm Lat and Shoulder Stretch 113
Exercise 60 — Full Body Extension 114

General Stretching Routines

Passive Muscle Assessment (PMA) .116
Reducing Lower Back Tension 118
Pre-and-Post Work Stretching Routine 120
3-Minute Office Stretching Routine 122

Sports Specific Stretching Routines

General Sports Stretching Routine .125
Ball Sports 126
Balance Sports 128
Golf Specific 130
Martial Arts 132
Racquet and Bat Sports 134
Running Specific 136
Swimming Specific 138

Photo & Illustration Credits

Cover Photo: Paul Collins/Mark Donaldson
Cover Design: Jens Vogelsang
Other Photos: Paul Collins

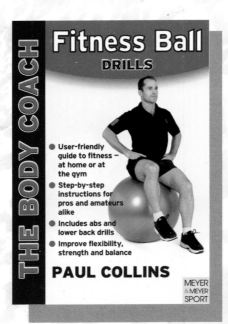